Faith and Fun

by

Kathleen M. Clark

MOORLEY'S Print & Publishing

© Copyright 1996

All rights reserved. No part of this publication may be reproduced, stored in a retrieval system, or transmitted, in any form or by any means, electronic, mechanical, photocopying, recording or otherwise, without the prior written permission of the publishers.

ISBN 0 86071 479 9

MOORLEY'S Print & Publishing
23 Park Rd., Ilkeston, Derbys DE7 5DA
Tel/Fax: (0115) 932 0643

Contents

A Child's Prayer	5
Hurrah for Santa Claus	6
Christmas Peace	6
William Booth	7
Peace in our time	8
Clever Grandpa	9
I do not fear the night	11
If only	11
If	11
Sunday School Picnic 1925	12
Sonnet	13
Back to school	13
Suffer the little children	14
Pity the little Centipede	14
Truth	15
Give me Peace in my heart	15
I'm a hungry Woodworm	16
Smile	16
Take me back to Lindisfarne	17
Friendship verses	18
Jamie's year	19
The Old Patchwork Quilt	21
There's always a rainbow	22
Play your part	22
Jesus took a Donkey	23
Heaven	23
A Place of Sweet Content	24
Have courage	24
I think that I met God today	25
Give thanks for Spring	25
The Lonely Pudding	26
Tell her you love her	27
The pouch	27
Ten boys from Sunday School	28
I thank my God	30
Ask yourself	31
We're in love	32
Gateways	33
These I love	34
The Innkeeper's lament	35

For
Simon David Roberts
with love

A CHILD'S PRAYER

God bless mummy. God bless dad
And bless me too I pray.
Help me to be a better boy
Than I was yesterday.

Let me be unselfish, Lord,
Not sneak the biggest bun.
Teach me not to tease the cat
Or pull its tail for fun.

I must not laugh when sister screams
And comes down in a rush.
I know the hedgehog in her bed
Is just a scrubbing brush.

I think it's very hard to be
A good boy like I should
I find that naughty tricks are fun.
Well, anybody would!

But when I say my prayers at night
And promise I will try
I hope that God is listening with
A twinkle in His eye.

HURRAH FOR SANTA CLAUS

Hurrah, hurrah, for Santa Claus
I asked him for a train
He brought me an electric one
Which dad has pinched again.

I set the rails out on the floor
A lovely long curved track
But dad has picked the engine up
And will not give it back.

Next Christmas I will ask my mum
To drop Santa a line
Tell him to bring my dad a train
So then he won't want mine.

CHRISTMAS PEACE

On that first Christmas morning
When Jesus Christ was born
The songs of waiting angels
Rang out to greet the dawn.

A cold dawn in a stable
A manger filled with hay
A Babe who came to teach us
The Life, the Truth, the Way.

So ring the bells at Christmas
And call the world to prove
Peace can be born at Christmas
Interpreted by Love.

WILLIAM BOOTH

Once, long ago, in Nottingham,
On a fine April morn
Down a narrow city street
A baby boy was born.

He loved to play in Sneinton fields
He skipped and jumped for joy
Mischievous, naughty, but not bad
A normal, loving boy.

And soon he gave his heart to God
Urged people to repent
And promise not to waste their lives
On selfish pleasure bent.

He went to London, tongue aflame,
To preach about God's Son
To tell men of the loving Lord
With time for everyone.

He worked among the down and outs
No soul too lost in sin
He worked to cast the devil out
And fought their love to win.

In Booth's Salvation Army
So many joined the ranks
The King and many a citizen
Had reason to give thanks.

When we remember William Booth
It should remind us all
How much one person can achieve
While answering God's call.

PEACE IN OUR TIME

Wise men may long in busy conference sit,
Eschew the use of arms and war estrange
As best they can.
Yet all is vain. No good may come of it
For laws are useless if they cannot change
The heart of man.

Who dares not rule by love defies God's plan;
The spleen of force turns in on self again,
Destroys the whole.
The iron bands of hate were forged by man
And only love may rob them of their pain
And heal each soul.

True peace is not an empty outward sham
It is a knowing in the inmost heart
That God is love.
It is a conscious living of Christ's life again
A joyous sharing of the truth love can impart
Or still may prove.

Clear down the years His gentle voice is heard
By those who seek yet cannot speak their need,
'My peace I give.
Go forward in my strength. Believe My word
That they who find Me shall be blessed indeed
And truly live.'

CLEVER GRANDPA

When Jamie woke up, oh so late,
And looked hard at the clock,
"You did not cuckoo, friend," he said,
"And Mummy did not knock."

"Oo," said the clock, "I could not speak
My throat is very sore
I know I didn't waken you
My error I deplore."

"Please hurry, Jamie," Mummy said,
"Your breakfast's getting cold
And if your clock is broken, dear,
Then Daddy must be told."

"I'm sorry Jamie," Daddy said,
"I have so much to do
I'll look at it when I get home
If that will comfort you."

The postman with his heavy sack
Had reached the garden gate
He said as Jamie ran to him,
"Come on, young man, you're late."

"Can you cure cuckoos with sore throats?"
Said Postie, "Cures are rare
If I could work such miracles
I'd be a millionaire."

The Milkman and the Coalman too
Gave similar advice
Try honey, lemon, glycerine
And lost of cooling ice.

But Mummy wouldn't let him try
She said, "They're teasing you
It needs an expert like Grandpa
To tell you what to do."

Jamie was feeling very sad
When Grandpa chanced to call
"Don't worry, Jamie, there's a cure
Which takes no time at all."

"We'll go together to the shop
And buy some special oil
Then Cuckoo Clock can swallow it
Those nasty germs to foil."

Glug! glug! the ailing Cuckoo Clock
Gulped down the soothing stuff
And when he found his voice again
Said Grandpa, "That's enough."

Now Jamie with a happy smile
Wakes early from his sleep
He knows his friend the Cuckoo Clock
Such perfect time will keep.

I DO NOT FEAR THE NIGHT

Oh help me, Saviour, every day
New strength in Thee to find.
My only just memorial
The love I leave behind.

Go with me through Gethsemane
I may not understand
But as the shadows lengthen, Lord,
Take thou my trembling hand.

So when my mind is stayed on Thee
And faith burns strangely bright
Then close the curtains gently, Lord,
I do not fear the night.

IF ONLY

I watched a snake slough off his skin
Down by a Yorkshire beck
If only I could do the same
I needn't wash my neck.
                    (Beck - a brook).

IF

If you've hurt someone whom you love
With an unguarded word
Or blackened someone's character
With spiteful tales you've heard
Then do not go to bed tonight
Until you've tried to put things right.

SUNDAY SCHOOL PICNIC 1925

Now Georgie will you please sit still
Until we reach the downs
There isn't room in this small cart
For sixteen would-be clowns.

Until we find the chosen spot
You children must be good.
Keep together. Don't get lost.
Behave as children should.

No Winnie, don't pull Sadie's plait
And Jack, she doesn't kiss
A boy who hasn't washed his face.
She's kept on saying this.

And Georgie if you must be sick
Tell me before you start
I'm sure you wouldn't want to spoil
The paint on this new cart.

Oh Mary, that was silly, dear,
To poke Tom in the eye
I know he tore your bonnet string
And pushed your hat awry.

Quite soon we'll all have sticky buns
And lots of hot sweet tea.
No Merle, you can't put brandy in.
Your mother does. I see.

Yes, Willie, all the sticky buns
Are roughly the same size
You can't have Jenny's. Give it back
And Jenny, wipe your eyes.

Now children, when we get you home
I hope that you will tell
Your aunts and uncles, parents too
The afternoon went well.

SONNET

The mangled breast of Mother Earth can save
No pap for half her sons - and so they die -
These little ones foredoomed at their first cry
To need no cradle but an empty grave.
A further boon than life itself they crave
While we, with rising passion question why
The seeming wise give credence to the lie
That they in step with power are doubly brave.
Why men so blinded by a love of power
Unseeing still usurp the gift of sight
And stumble down the path that men have trod
And will retread until that finer hour
When they, like moths bedazzled by the light,
Turn baffled back to their beginning - God.

BACK TO SCHOOL

The children gone - I feel the peace
Seep silently through every room.
A longed-for quiet now is mine.
(Should it remind me of a tomb?)

The clock ticks on - the hours drag
I wander round the empty place
Clear up their toys and then regret
The unaccustomed, spotless space.

Excited footsteps down the road
Soon make my flagging spirits soar
Then my heart sings - they're home again
I hurry to fling wide the door.

SUFFER THE LITTLE CHILDREN

The young are timeless
They are a common trust
An immortality
The world must cherish.

Who so offends
These little ones
Shall perish from the land
Leaving no sign.

In them the past and present meet
They are the synthesis of time
Fulfilment of our yesterdays
Tomorrow's promise
And the reason
For our striving.

With them we must keep faith
For in their living
Life pays its fee to us
And we are rich
Beyond the wealth of kings.

PITY THE LITTLE CENTIPEDE

Pity the little centipede
Who has so many feet
He's very busy cleaning shoes
He has no time to eat.

Pity the little centipede
Who hated to admit
Shoe sixty nine is pinching me
But all the others fit.

TRUTH

Deep in a dusty acorn
A mighty oak lies curled
Locked in a newborn baby's mind
The future of the world.

Safe in a grain of ripening wheat
Man's sustenance in store
And in his trusting love of God
His life for evermore.

GIVE ME PEACE IN MY HEART

Give me peace in my heart, oh God,
When the busy day is done.
Let me rest in the knowledge that,
I am your well-loved Son.

Give me strength to go on, Oh God,
Bruised and battered and sore.
Forgiving each slight and scorning the spite,
Keeping no account of the score.

Give me discernment, God, to see,
The pain behind another's smile.
With souls long seared by loneliness,
To go the second mile.

Give me a great concern, oh God,
For others along the way
Then lead me gently back to Thee
The life, the Truth, the Way.

I'M A HUNGRY WOODWORM

I'm a hungry woodworm
Chewing lots of wood.
The doctor said to spit it out
I only wish I could.

I'm a hungry woodworm
Making sawdust fast.
Out of chairs and chests of drawers
Which men had built to last.

I'm a hungry woodworm
One day I'm sure I'll choke.
On breakfasts of mahogany
And dinners of light oak.

I'm a hungry woodworm
Please spare a thought for me.
When you are having fruit and cream
I've only wood for tea.

So if I chew the pulpit up
Maybe attack the roof.
It goes to show how starved I am
If you should need the proof.

SMILE!

If you have missed the sunshine
And wished for it in vain
Remember in life's garden
That flowers need the rain.
There never was a storm-cloud
That did not melt away
So smile while you are waiting
And brighten someone's day.

TAKE ME BACK TO LINDISFARNE

Take me back to Lindisfarne
Cradle of our Christian faith.
Where the cotton grasses bend
In the salt-filled breeze.

Let me see again
The brooding hump of Mullach Mor
Sulking in mist
And hear the sad sigh of the sea
On tear-wet, shingled shore.

Let me not forget
The young seals' pleading eyes
Begging men's mercy
Pre-doomed to disappointment.
Keep me from harm
Where cord grass tangles
On the lonely dunes
Sucking the soil life
From pink sea thrift.

Above, the short-eared owl
Waited in his solitary tree
Tensed and silent
While a shivering field vole
Cowered in a world
Grown cold with nameless fear.

Here when evening folds
The tired world to rest
The Priory Church
Pearled in moonlight
Reminds me that eternal values
Laugh at Time's advance.

FRIENDSHIP VERSES

What is true happiness, you ask.
A larger house, a bigger car,
Or jewellery, expensive clothes -
No, there are finer things by far.

The sweetness of a baby's kiss,
The loving smile of spouse or friend,
No greater happiness than this
To bring content at each day's end.

Just one smile
Can make another's day
Just one star
Can cheer the darkest way
Just one word
Can banish loneliness
Just one hope
Can point you to success.

Now whether you are rich or poor
You will have things to share
You need not head subscription lists
To show you really care.
If you can smile, extend a hand,
To help a lonely soul
Kindness will grow by constant use
And permeate the whole.

JAMIE'S YEAR

Remember all years have twelve months
Each brings a special joy
To brighten up the daily lives
Of every girl and boy.

In January the days are short
But Jamie hopes for snow
It's great to slip and slide and sledge
While feet and fingers glow.

In February when days are dull
He watches raindrops run
All down the window pane and longs
For puddle-splashing fun.

Mad March blows and brings the gales
He thinks of ships at sea
And wonders what it's really like
To be tossed constantly.

April arrives with sun and rain
These two bring the flowers
His Mummy loves the daffodils
That brighten Springtime hours.

In May the lazy cuckoo calls
She's searching for a nest
Where some-one else will hatch her egg
Then she can have a rest.

In June most birds are rearing young
And working hard and long
To give their babies all they need
So they'll grow big and strong.

July comes in with fine warm days
And Jamie's by the sea
He's finding seashells in rock pools
Collecting them with glee.

August arrives and Grandpa comes
(Sometimes his dog as well!)
Long stories of the olden days
He really loves to tell.

September means some birds depart
To lands across the sea
Where they will miss the icy winds
When we feel shivery.

October spreads a coloured rug
Of leaves beneath the trees
How Jamie loves to rustle them
They dance in every breeze.

November comes with fog and mist
And Jamie stays inside
While Mummy tells him lovely tales
Of countries far and wide.

December brings good Christmas cheer
And presents by the tree
Exciting parties still to come
Before next January.

Now the Old Year slips away
And vanishes in space
So silently and happily
The New Year takes its place.

THE OLD PATCHWORK QUILT

The loving hands that stitched this quilt
Are long since dead and gone
But in each coloured square, grandma,
Your happiness lives on.

The silk that forms the centre square
Was from your wedding gown
A union that four fine sons
Three daughters too would crown.

The white lawn from a baby's dress
Your firstborn grandchild wore
Each stitch a token of your love
No babe could ask for more.

Now, Grandma, you do not need your quilt
No noise your last rest mars
You sleep in perfect peace beneath
An eiderdown of stars.

THERE'S ALWAYS A RAINBOW

The thunder rolls
Round distant hills
Torrential rain
Each river fills.

The sodden birds
Seek shelter then
The wise old owl
The fragile wren.

Keen gardeners
Tie up and stake
So flowers bend
But do not break.

A rainbow arcs
Across the plain
Children come out
To play again.

❖ ❖ ❖ ❖ ❖ ❖ ❖ ❖

PLAY YOUR PART

You may not put the world to rights
But you can do your part
And brighten your small corner up
The perfect place to start.
For you can live for others
Their joys and sorrows share
Help where you can by word and deed
To show you really care.

❖ ❖ ❖ ❖ ❖ ❖ ❖ ❖

JESUS TOOK A DONKEY

Shaggy grey donkey
Of ancient fame
Derided by men
No-one can name.

Carrying the Master
How felt you then
Steadily bearing
The Lord of men?

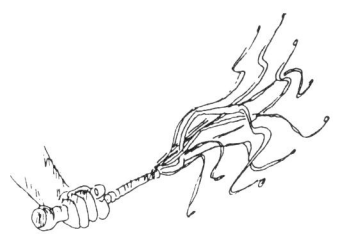

Little grey donkey
Humble and meek
Yours was the honour
All Christians seek.

Let us then gently
Serve God and pray
We, too, may meet Jesus
On life's rough way.

HEAVEN

Not for me the busy roads
With all their dust and noise
Down leafy lanes in quiet ways
There lie my special joys.

Oh, not for me the city's grime
Or its demanding voice
I find my ease in flower-flecked fields
They make my heart rejoice.

And not for me the neon lights
Men crave for constantly
Fresh dewdrops sparkling in the sun
These are true wealth to me.

The warmth of kindly neighbours' smiles
Friends' trust so freely given
In kindnesses performed with love
Lies my idea of Heaven.

A PLACE OF SWEET CONTENT

No satin sheets or porcelain cups
No central heating there
No fancy food or silver knives
Just homely, loving care.

Clean beds that smell of lavender
A welcome and a smile
Make grandma's cottage, just the place
To stay and rest awhile.

A haven from the bustling world
Where happy days are spent
With one whose wisdom makes her home
A place of sweet content.

HAVE COURAGE

Did you know a sunbeam
Was resting by a rill
When Mother Nature changed it to
A golden daffodil?

So if you're feeling useless
And wondering what to do
Tell Jesus you are hoping that
He has a plan for you.

And when it is revealed
Have courage then to say
How blest I am to have the strength
To serve you, Lord, today.

I THINK THAT I MET GOD TODAY

I think that I met God today,
Not in a crowded church,
But in a garden's solitude,
Beneath a silver birch.

I think that I saw God today,
In faces of fresh flowers,
Who only served to pleasure me,
Through this day's sunlit hours.

I think that I heard God today,
In a small bird's happy song,
Which lifted spirits, cheered sad hearts,
Lasted the whole day long.

I thank you, God, for these your gifts,
And for your loving care,
Help me to show a real concern,
For people everywhere.

GIVE THANKS FOR SPRING

Spring scatters daisies in the grass
Pink-tipped they open as I pass.
She tells each bird to build a nest
And teaches it to sing its best.
She asks the leaves to dress the trees
Before they dance in each cool breeze.
She laughs as windflowers star the shade
Commands bluebells to mist the glade.
And as my heart with pleasure fills
She brings the golden daffodils.

THE LONELY PUDDING

I'm a lonely Yorkshire Pudding
Who doesn't want to rise
I'm sitting sadly in my tin
With fat tears in my eyes.

Yes, I've been sitting in this place
In swirls of melting fat
For hours and hours since morning broke
I'm not enjoying that.

I didn't mind being battered hard
With an enormous whisk
I didn't mind being flattened like
A giant floppy disc.

But as the heat is rising
I mind it very much
That my sit-upon is burning
And crumbling at a touch.

So when you put a pudding
In an oven which is hot
Just leave it on the middle shelf
Where the hottest heat is not.

TELL HER YOU LOVE HER

When did you tell your mother,
Your love is warm and true.
And how much you appreciate,
Her constant care of you?

Or do you take for granted now,
Her selfless service too.
Her loyalty and firm support,
That's always there for you.

Just ask yourself where would you be,
Today without her aid.
Tell her before it is too late,
The difference she has made.

THE POUCH

'Empty your mouth,' my mother said,
'Before you eat more bread.
For if you don't you'll hear me say,
Go straight upstairs to bed.'

'Well, Hammy Hamster eats and eats,
His cheeks both bulge with food.
If I do that you quickly say,
That I am very rude.'

'Yes, dear, but Hammy has a special pouch
As you have heard me tell.'
'I know but wouldn't it be jolly good,
If I had one as well.'

TEN BOYS FROM SUNDAY SCHOOL

Ten boys from Sunday School
Standing in a line
One forgot to say amen
Then there were nine.

Nine boys from Sunday School
All prepared to wait
One left his bible home
Then there were eight.

Eight boys from Sunday School
Thought they were in Heaven
When one produced some chewing gum
Then there were seven.

Seven boys from Sunday School
All were in a fix
One didn't know who Adam was
Then there were six.

Six boys from Sunday School
Hoping to survive
One lost his bus fare home
Then there were five.

Five boys from Sunday School
Adding up their score
The teacher said, 'Collection, please'
Then there were four.

Four boys from Sunday School
Carolled lustily
Till one forgot King Wenceslas
Then there were three.

Three boys from Sunday School
Each was in a stew
When one was asked to sing top doh
Then there were two.

Two boys from Sunday School
Longed to have some fun
One got bored and went to sleep
Then there was one.

One boy from Sunday School
Said, 'This won't do at all.'
When he phoned, the other nine
Responded to his call.

Ten boys from Sunday School
Decided to be good
They listened and they learnt a lot
As wise folk said they would.

N.B. This poem may be performed by ten small children each one capable of remembering one verse. The line of ten gradually disappears only to emerge intact for the final verse.

I THANK MY GOD

For mother's love, for father's care
For kindly people everywhere
I thank my God.

For mists of bluebells in the glade
For every stately oak tree's shade
I thank my God.

For the sound of babbling brooks
For primroses in mossy nooks
I thank my God.

For dewdrops glinting on the grass
For birdsong rising as I pass
I thank my God.

For friendships lasting down the years
For those who stay to calm my fears
I thank my God.

For every unexpected smile
For those who go the second mile
I thank my God.

For comfort through the darkest night
When new hope comes with morning light
Oh God, I thank Thee.

ASK YOURSELF

Why did you go to church today?
To show off your new dress?
Why did you seek out a front seat
The others to impress?

Why did you put a ten pound note
On the collection plate?
Was it because you had refused
The beggar at your gate?

Why did you send your injured friend
The biggest bunch of flowers?
Had you neglected to ring up
Or put it off for hours?

Why did you give permission to
Fix up a bedside phone?
Was it to compensate your son
For hours he spends alone.

When you decide what you will do
And confidence is high
In spite of what the world may think
Take time to wonder why.

WE'RE IN LOVE

He never puts his clothes away
Just leaves them on a chair
Blames me when they get crumpled up
It really is not fair
But I don't mind
Cos we're in love.

He never washes round the bath
Just leaves a tide-mark there
Then splashes everything in sight
And doesn't seem to care.
But I don't mind
Cos we're in love.

I always let the eggs boil hard
My pastry's harder still
I can't make bread or fairy cakes
I'm sure I never will
But he won't mind
Cos we're in love.

I never do arrive on time
My birthday cards are late
We got married in the Spring
I just forget the date.
But we don't mind
Cos love is great.

GATEWAYS

It stands there still
A wooden gate,
Swinging on its hinge.
I see a merry, laughing child
With golden curls and fringe.

It stands there still
An open gate,
A young girl rushes out
Impatient for excitement now
Undeterred by doubt.

It stands there still
A painted gate,
Wide open for a bride
I glimpse her eager shining face
Her husband by her side.

It stands there still
A creaking gate
Through long, golden days
Spent among the welcome flowers
Down quiet sunlit ways.

THESE I LOVE

The primrose with her candid face
The windflower with its easy grace.

The shadiness of stately trees
The freshness of the gentle breeze.

The golden catkins hanging low
The fragile snowdrop white as snow.

The merry chuckle of the brook
The throaty call of circling rook.

The apple cheek of country lass
The pink-tipped daisy in the grass.

The soothing warmth of summer sun
The quietude when day is done.
All these I love.

THE INNKEEPER'S LAMENT

If only I had known
The blessed Saviour of the world
Was waiting to be born
I would have cleared a space
Offered my warmest room
If only I had known.

If only I had known
The mother of the Holy Babe
Was asking me for help
I would have left my wine
To tend her every need
If only I had known.

If only I had known
That all the panoply of Heaven
And angels hovered near
I would have worshipped Him
On humble, bended knee
If only I had known!

MOORLEY'S are growing Publishers, adding several new titles to our list each year. We also undertake private publications and commissioned works.

Our range of publications includes: **Books of Verse**
Devotional Poetry
Recitations
Drama
Bible Plays
Sketches
Nativity Plays
Passiontide Plays
Easter Plays
Demonstrations
Resource Books
Assembly Material
Songs & Musicals
Children's Addresses
Prayers & Graces
Daily Readings
Books for Speakers
Activity Books
Quizzes
Puzzles
Painting Books
Daily Readings
Church Stationery
Notice Books
Cradle Rolls
Hymn Board Numbers

Please send a S.A.E. (approx 9" x 6") for the current catalogue or consult your local Christian Bookshop who should stock or be able to order our titles.